"JESUS LOVES ME"
Prayer Journal

RAYSHELLE RICHARDSON

Quantum Discovery
A LITERARY AGENCY

ISBN
978-1-964982-71-7 (Paperback)
978-1-964982-72-4 (eBook)

Nothing will be able to separate us from the Love of God that is in Christ Jesus.

Romans 8:39

Presented to

_____

Today I Praise and thank God For:

How good it is to sing praises to our God, Psalm: 147:1

Today I ask God for:

By Prayer and petition, with thanksgiving, present your request to God, Philippians 4:6

Reflection/expression

I am awesomely and wonderfully made.
Psalm 139:14 NASB

Today I Praise and thank God For:

How good it is to sing praises to our God, Psalm: 147:1

Today I ask God for:

By Prayer and petition, with thanksgiving, present your request to God, Philippians 4:6

Reflection/expression

We know and rely on the love God has for us.
1 John 4:16 NIV

Today I Praise and thank God For:

How good it is to sing praises to our God, Psalm: 147:1

Today I ask God for:

By Prayer and petition, with thanksgiving, present your request to God, Philippians 4:6

Reflection/expression

The Lord is my shepherd, I will not be in need.
Psalm 23:1 NASB

Today I Praise and thank God For:

How good it is to sing praises to our God, Psalm: 147:1

Today I ask God for:

By Prayer and petition, with thanksgiving, present your request to God, Philippians 4:6

Reflection/expression

We love because He first loved us.
1 John 4:19 NASB

Today I Praise and thank God For:

How good it is to sing praises to our God, Psalm: 147:1

Today I ask God for:

By Prayer and petition, with thanksgiving, present your request to God, Philippians 4:6

Reflection/expression

You will protect me from trouble.
Psalm 32:7 NIV

Today I Praise and thank God For:

How good it is to sing praises to our God, Psalm: 147:1

Today I ask God for:

By Prayer and petition, with thanksgiving, present your request to God, Philippians 4:6

Reflection/expression

Let the morning bring me word of your unfailing love.

Psalm143:8 NIV

Today I Praise and thank God For:

How good it is to sing praises to our God, Psalm: 147:1

Today I ask God for:

By Prayer and petition, with thanksgiving, present your request to God, Philippians 4:6

Reflection/expression

Do not be afraid or discouraged, for the Lord
your God will be with you wherever you go.
Joshua 1:9 NIV

Today I Praise and thank God For:

How good it is to sing praises to our God, Psalm: 147:1

Today I ask God for:

By Prayer and petition, with thanksgiving, present your request to God, Philippians 4:6

Reflection/expression

A new command I give you, Love one another as I have Loved you.

John 13:34 NIV

Today I Praise and thank God For:

How good it is to sing praises to our God, Psalm: 147:1

Today I ask God for:

By Prayer and petition, with thanksgiving, present your request to God, Philippians 4:6

Reflection/expression

Praise be to the God and Father of our Lord Jesus Christ, who has Blessed us with every Spiritual Blessing.
Ephesians 1:3 NIV

Today I Praise and thank God For:

How good it is to sing praises to our God, Psalm: 147:1

Today I ask God for:

By Prayer and petition, with thanksgiving, present your request to God, Philippians 4:6

Reflection/expression

May you be fully capable ofcomprehending how long and high and deep is the Love of Christ. Ephesians 3:18 NIV

Today I Praise and thank God For:

How good it is to sing praises to our God, Psalm: 147:1

Today I ask God for:

By Prayer and petition, with thanksgiving, present your request to God, Philippians 4:6

Reflection/expression

The Lord is faithful, He will strengthen you and
protect you from the evil one.
2 Thessalonians 3:3 NIV

Today I Praise and thank God For:

How good it is to sing praises to our God, Psalm: 147:1

Today I ask God for:

By Prayer and petition, with thanksgiving, present your request to God, Philippians 4:6

Reflection/expression

Give thanks to the Lord, for He is good, His Love endures forever.
1 Chronicles 16:34 NIV

Today I Praise and thank God For:

How good it is to sing praises to our God, Psalm: 147:1

Today I ask God for:

By Prayer and petition, with thanksgiving, present your request to God, Philippians 4:6

Reflection/expression

The righteous person faces many troubles, but
the Lord comes to the rescue each time.
Psalm 34:19 NIV

Today I Praise and thank God For:

How good it is to sing praises to our God, Psalm: 147:1

Today I ask God for:

By Prayer and petition, with thanksgiving, present your request to God, Philippians 4:6

Reflection/expression

May the Lord direct your hearts into the Love of God and into the patience of Christ.
2 Thessalonians 3:5 ASV

Today I Praise and thank God For:

How good it is to sing praises to our God, Psalm: 147:1

Today I ask God for:

By Prayer and petition, with thanksgiving, present your request to God, Philippians 4:6

Reflection/expression

I will strengthen you and help you, I will hold you up with my righteous right hand.
Isaiah 41:10 NIV

Today I Praise and thank God For:

How good it is to sing praises to our God, Psalm: 147:1

Today I ask God for:

By Prayer and petition, with thanksgiving, present your request to God, Philippians 4:6

Reflection/expression

For God has not given us a spirit of fear and timidity, but of power, love and sound mind.
2 Timothy 1:7 KJV

Today I Praise and thank God For:

How good it is to sing praises to our God, Psalm: 147:1

Today I ask God for:

By Prayer and petition, with thanksgiving, present your request to God, Philippians 4:6

Reflection/expression

I will never leave you, I will never forsake you.
Hebrews 13:5 NIV

Today I Praise and thank God For:

How good it is to sing praises to our God, Psalm: 147:1

Today I ask God for:

By Prayer and petition, with thanksgiving, present your request to God, Philippians 4:6

Reflection/expression

The mountains may be shaken and the hills be removed, but my faithful love for you will remain.
Isaiah 54:10 NIV

Today I Praise and thank God For:

How good it is to sing praises to our God, Psalm: 147:1

Today I ask God for:

By Prayer and petition, with thanksgiving, present your request to God, Philippians 4:6

Reflection/expression

May the LORD answer you when you are in trouble.

Psalm 20:1 NASB

Today I Praise and thank God For:

How good it is to sing praises to our God, Psalm: 147:1

Today I ask God for:

By Prayer and petition, with thanksgiving, present your request to God, Philippians 4:6

Reflection/expression

The Great love of the Lord never fails.
Lamentations 3:22 NIV

Today I Praise and thank God For:

How good it is to sing praises to our God, Psalm: 147:1

Today I ask God for:

By Prayer and petition, with thanksgiving, present your request to God, Philippians 4:6

Reflection/expression

My God will supply all your needs.
Philippians 4:19 ASV

Today I Praise and thank God For:

How good it is to sing praises to our God, Psalm: 147:1

Today I ask God for:

By Prayer and petition, with thanksgiving, present your request to God, Philippians 4:6

Reflection/expression

Your unfailing love is better than life itself.
Psalm 63:3 NIV

Today I Praise and thank God For:

How good it is to sing praises to our God, Psalm: 147:1

Today I ask God for:

By Prayer and petition, with thanksgiving, present your request to God, Philippians 4:6

Reflection/expression

My God is my rock, in whom I take refuge.
2 Samuel 22:3 NIV

Today I Praise and thank God For:

How good it is to sing praises to our God, Psalm: 147:1

Today I ask God for:

By Prayer and petition, with thanksgiving, present your request to God, Philippians 4:6

Reflection/expression

He is the faithful God, keeping His covenant of love to a thousand generations. Deuteronomy 7:9 NIV

Today I Praise and thank God For:

How good it is to sing praises to our God, Psalm: 147:1

Today I ask God for:

By Prayer and petition, with thanksgiving, present your request to God, Philippians 4:6

Reflection/expression

The LORD keeps you from all harm and watches over your life.
Psalm 121: 7 NIV

Today I Praise and thank God For:

How good it is to sing praises to our God, Psalm: 147:1

Today I ask God for:

By Prayer and petition, with thanksgiving, present your request to God, Philippians 4:6

Reflection/expression

For God so loved the world that He gave his one and only Son, so whoever believes in him will not perish but have eternal life.
John 3:16

www.ingramcontent.com/pod-product-compliance
Lightning Source LLC
Chambersburg PA
CBHW041542120626
46551CB00019B/2798